PEARL HARBOR

IMAGES OF AN AMERICAN MEMORIAL

Allan Seiden

Mutual Publishing

ISBN-10: 1-56647-714-X
ISBN-13: 978-1-56647-714-7
Library of Congress Catalog Card Number: 2005921655

First Printing, May 2005
Second Printing, September 2007
Third Printing, January 2011
Fourth Printing, April 2013
Fifth Printing, May 2015
Sixth Printing, March 2017

Mutual Publishing, LLC
1215 Center Street, Suite 210
Honolulu, Hawai'i 96816
Ph: 808-732-1709 / Fax: 808-734-4094
Email: info@mutualpublishing.com
www.mutualpublishing.com

Printed in Taiwan

Dedication

Dedicated to those who serve their country in a time of need and specifically to those for whom Pearl Harbor proved a final resting place.

Introduction

Few places register as profound an impact as Pearl Harbor. Today, many years after Japan unleashed what President Franklin Roosevelt memorably called "a date of infamy," Pearl Harbor resonates not only for the generation that lived through it, but for their children, grandchildren and great-grandchildren. If anything, the horrific attack on the World Trade Center on 9/11 has given new meaning to what occurred on December 7, 1941.

That Sunday morning began under clear, sunny skies, thoughts of awakening military personnel likely focused on the weekend's escapades. There was talk that Pearl Harbor, home of America's Pacific Fleet, was a likely target should war break out. But a tenuous peace prevailed, and few thought the threat to be imminent. America's focus was on Europe, where Hitler's successful aggressions were a pressing cause for alarm.

Logic affirmed that Hawai'i was at risk, although the islands' isolation seemed to afford protection from attack. More than four thousand miles to the east, Japan did not seem capable of inflicting a devastating attack on Hawai'i. There was no precedent for the impressive logistical feat accomplished by the Japanese transfer of a full attack force, including more than four hundred well-equipped fighter planes, to within two hundred miles of O'ahu.

Some precautions had been implemented to protect military installations on O'ahu. Battleships and military aircraft had been concentrated to protect against sabotage, for example. That very precaution made them sitting ducks when Japanese planes came swarming over O'ahu from the north in two aerial attacks that would devastate America's military defenses. When, at about 7:30 A.M., planes were spotted approaching O'ahu on a newly installed Army radar screen, the report was dismissed, the radar sighting assumed to be a squadron due in from California that morning. By 7:52 A.M. the truth would hit home as the first bombs hit Wheeler

Airfield, followed by attacks on the 'Ewa Marine Station and Ford Island. A second attack began at 8:40 A.M..

By 10 A.M. it was all over. The damage inflicted was massive, with facilities ablaze, eight battleships destroyed or disabled, 164 planes destroyed and another 159 damaged, 2,390 dead, and thousands more wounded. Fires raged, forming dark columns of grey-black smoke that rose over Pearl Harbor and five other military installations around the island. But the strike had missed its primary objective, the Pacific Fleet's aircraft carriers, which were out of port at the time of the attack. The attacking planes also failed to destroy the fuel storage facilities at Hickam Airfield, adjacent to Pearl Harbor. That allowed America a rapid response, ultimately denying Japan the advantages it sought in launching a surprise attack. Just as significantly, the attack galvanized the nation, providing a powerful rallying point for the country's rapid mobilization.

The rebuilding of damaged facilities and ships started immediately, with the harbor quickly rehabilitated and most of the damaged ships repaired and restored to service. Fate would not be so kind to the battleships USS *Utah*, USS *Oklahoma* and USS *Arizona*, all damaged beyond repair. The USS *Arizona*, with 1,177 dead, most still aboard their sunken ship, came to symbolize the war effort.

The USS *Arizona* Memorial, built atop a sunken hull of the battleship, continues to provide a stirring symbol of the national effort that followed the attack on Pearl Harbor. The USS *Arizona* Memorial Visitor Center, operated by the National Park Service, provides a meaningful introduction to a visit to the Memorial.

The pages that follow provide a glimpse of what happened on December 7, 1941. They reveal why Pearl Harbor remains a place that evokes profound feelings and food for thought.

A view of Pearl Harbor, c. 1825. The harbor's shallow waters attracted Polynesians who built many fishponds along its meandering shores. The Hawaiians had names for different sections of the harbor, which was most frequently referred to as Pu'uloa, or long hill. The English name refers to a now-extinct pearl oyster once common to its waters.

King Kalākaua (inset). During Kalākaua's reign the U.S. won extra territorial rights to Pearl Harbor. One of the first facilities built was a coaling station for naval ships.

By 1915 military facilities included dry docks (above right) and berthing docks for the fleet's battleships (above left).

1937. Japanese officers parading before their troops in China. Japan's militaristic orientation, fanatically adhered to and brutally carried out, made an apocalyptic war inevitable.

Emperor Hirohito reviewing troops. Considered a god by his people, Emperor Hirohito had only limited control of the government of the country he ruled. Militaristic generals forged an aggressive policy designed to establish Japan as a major world power.

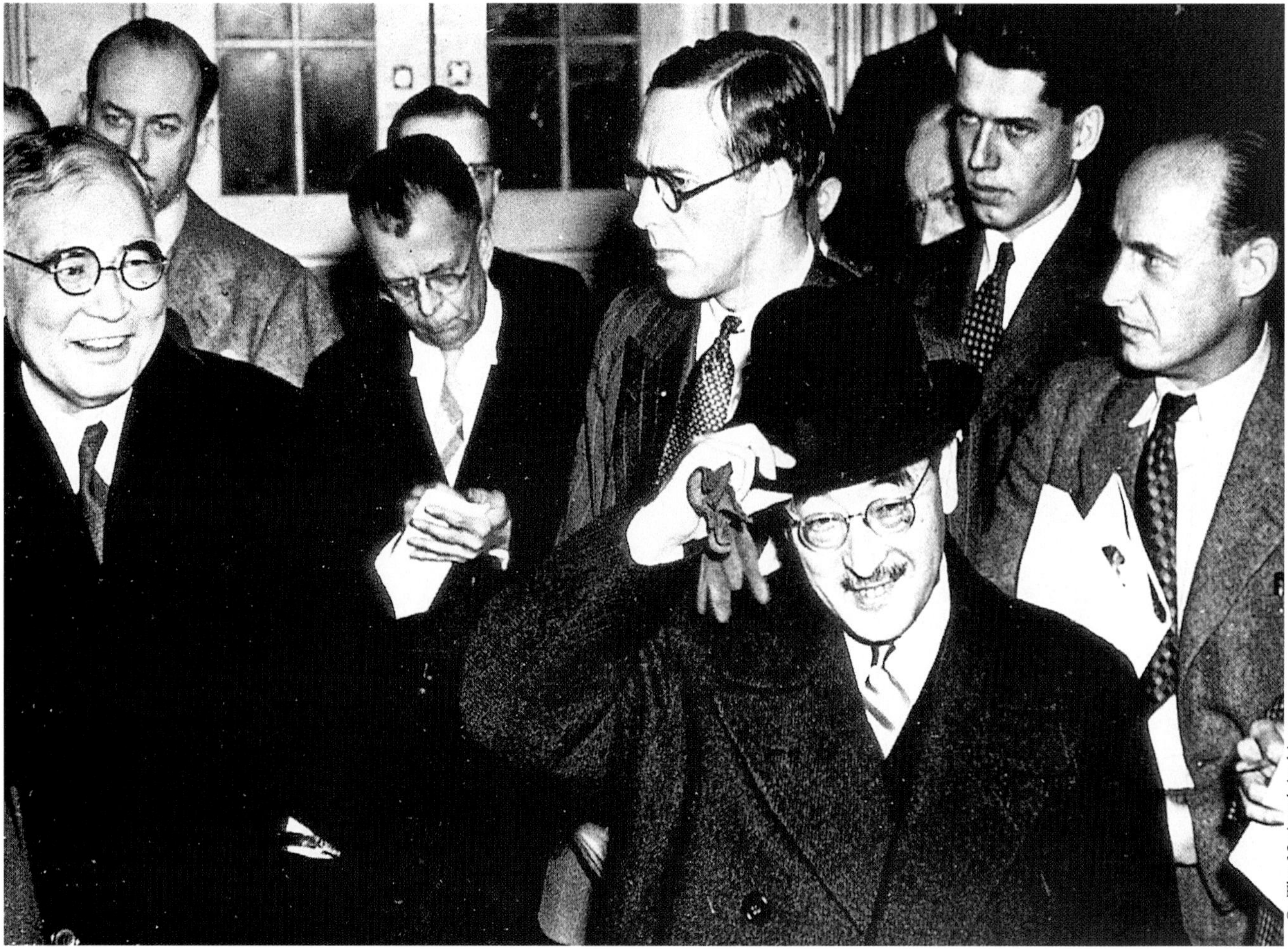

© The National Archives

Diplomacy, masking the intended attack, continued in Washington between U.S. Secretary of State Cordell Hull and Japanese envoys Nomura (left) and Kurusu (right). The attack was to have been timed to follow delivery of a note declaring war. Late delivery of the note resulted in the attack preceding the declaration of war.

Pilots rev up their engine in a precision dry run en route to Hawai'i.

Part of the Japanese fleet, with Mt. Fuji as a backdrop, c. 1939.

Battleships of the Pacific Fleet at anchor in Pearl Harbor,
in silhouette against the Waiʻanae Mountains, c. 1940.

The Japanese Kate high-level bomber, photographed over Hickam Airfield, adjacent to Pearl Harbor, was the most lethal weapon in the attack. Bombers attacked in two waves, hitting six military installations on O'ahu.

Pearl Harbor from the air, 1941. Ford Island, with its wide airstrip, lies at the center, battleships clustered offshore. Hickam Airfield lies just beyond the fuel storage tanks on the east shore.

Battleship Row, December 7, 1941. A plume of smoke rises above Hickam Airfield.
Ripples in the water identify torpedoes en route to direct hits on the battleship USS *Oklahoma*
(top ship, second from right) and the neighboring USS *West Virginia*.

From 'Aiea Heights, the waters of the East Loch are afire, Battleship Row covered in dense smoke.

The flag still flies from the bow of the stricken USS *West Virginia*.

The view from the east shore reveals Pearl Harbor ablaze.

Fires raged for more than two days, adding to the damage and the difficulty confronting rescue teams. Two hours after the attack the USS *Arizona* continued to send up clouds of black smoke, caused by burning fuel that coated the harbor's waters.

Hickam Airfield is in flames after a 90-minute-long series of attacks.
Luckily fuel storage tanks adjacent to the airfield were not hit.

Smoke rises from the Army's Wheeler Field, which lost fifty-three planes in the attack. The Navy, Marine and Army Air Corps were decimated in attacks at six military airfields on Oʻahu. Only a few American aircraft were able to take to the skies by the time a second wave of planes bombed the island, most were destroyed as they tried to gain altitude.

24

© The National Archives

The second aerial attack began at 8:40 A.M., just minutes after the first attacking planes, having released their cargo of bombs, headed back to their home ships. Longer than the first assault, the second attack force of 167 planes proved equally disastrous, hitting airfields and bases around Oʻahu. By 10 A.M. the last Japanese planes had left Hawaiian skies, leaving behind a stricken fleet and a shocked nation.

Moored next to each other, the USS *Tennessee* and the USS *West Virginia* were hit by torpedoes and aerial bombs. Both ships were repaired and returned to service in the Pacific.

War is declared: President Roosevelt addresses a joint session of the U.S. Congress
on December 8, detailing events and requesting a declaration of war on the Empire of Japan.
The attack united the nation for the five years it took to defeat Japan.

The USS *Arizona* in Pearl Harbor's calm waters in the 1930s.
Completed in 1918, she was modernized twice in the 1930s.

The USS *Arizona*'s newly modernized galley, c.1935, was designed to handle more than 5,000 meals served daily to the 1,731 men aboard.

© USS *Arizona* Memorial/NPS Photo Collection

Eight direct bomb hits doomed the USS *Arizona*, engulfing its foremast and bridge in flames and smoke.

© The National Archives

Oil fires raged for two days, leaving behind twisted wreckage.
Much of the above-water sections of the ships were removed and recycled.

© Hawai'i State Archives

Clean-up and rescue crews worked round-the-clock to contain oil fires.
Fire hoses are aimed at the still-burning USS *West Virginia* following the second attack.

In addition to battleships, numerous other classes of ships were damaged. The destroyers USS *Downes* (left) and USS *Cassin*, damaged beyond repair by aerial bombs and depth charges while in dry-dock, were dismantled for scrap in 1942. The more moderately damaged battleship USS *Pennsylvania* remains afloat behind the destroyers.

Rescue teams approach the capsized battleship USS *Oklahoma*. Righted after a two-year-long rescue effort, the USS *Oklahoma* proved too badly damaged to be returned to service.

The twisted remains of the USS *Shaw*.

The attack on Pearl Harbor shocked, enraged and galvanized the nation, providing motivation and a slogan that has survived the war: "Remember Pearl Harbor!"

Honolulu Star-Bulletin 3rd EXTRA

8 PAGES—HONOLULU, TERRITORY OF HAWAII, U. S. A., SUNDAY, DECEMBER 7, 1941—8 PAGES ★★★ PRICE FIVE

MARTIAL LAW DECLARED
DEATHS ARE MOUNTING
OVER 400 KILLED HERE; JAPAN ANNOUNCES "WAR
Japanese Raids On Guam, Panama Are Reporte
Oahu Blackout Tonight; Fleet Here Moves Out to S

Our Waves, Start 7:55, Oahu Hit Many Places

BULLETIN

By The Associated Press

), Dec. 7.—Imperial headquarters announced at tonight that Japan had entered a state of war United States and Great Britain in the western om dawn today.

Governor Proclaims National Emergency

Governor Poindexter said he would make a full report to President Roosevelt of the bombing attacks on Honolulu by radiophone immediately after his radio message to the people of Honolulu.

The governor said at 11:30 that there had been no evidence of sabotage by local Japanese residents.

Governor Poindexter this morning issued the following proclamation declaring a defense period to exist throughout the territory; thereby putting into effect the provisions of the M-Day act of the special session of the legislature:

"Under and by virtue of the powers vested in me by Act 24 of the special session laws of Hawaii, 1941, and particularly Section 5 thereof, and under by virtue of all powers in me vested by law, I, J. B. Poindexter, governor of the territory of Hawaii, do hereby find that a state of affairs ex-

MARTIAL LAW

Lt. General Walter C. Short, commanding general of the Hawaiian department, issued the following statement at 3:45 p. m. today:

"Governor Poindexter has just proclaimed martial law. All civilian governmental agencies will continue to function under the governor.

"Today the Hawaiian islands were attacked by Japanese airplanes.

"Although a state of war exists, the civilian population of these islands has reacted in a

The afternoon paper on December 7 headlines the immediate implementation of martial law. That meant military police, curfews, blackout windows and ration cards amongst other things. For most people, a sense of common purpose trumped the inconveniences of the war years.

© Hawaiian Legacy Archive

38

Hula girls welcome a battleship back to port in 1943. As headquarters of the Pacific war, Hawai'i provided rest and recreation for troops in the Pacific theater.

© Hawai'i State Archives

1943. Searchlights light up the night sky, heralding Pearl Harbor's triumph over the devastating attack.

A combination of military and civilian work crews, men and women, worked to restore the harbor and the damaged Pacific Fleet.

1943. A portion of the Pacific Fleet, rebuilt and expanded.
After the attack, battleships were anchored further apart and in open water.

The war over, the battleship USS *Missouri* enters Hawaiian waters, 1945.

The Battleship USS *Missouri* at anchor off Ford Island, to the left the USS *Arizona* Memorial, and the Ford Island Bridge. Hickam lies across the East Loch from the USS *Missouri*.

© Allan Seiden

Remembrance Circle, part of the USS *Arizona* Memorial Visitor Center,
with tablets that record the casualties of the attack. (inset) Exterior view, USS *Arizona* Memorial Visitor Center.

The USS *Arizona* Memorial rises above the sunken hull of the battleship it honors. Most of the 1,177 men who perished aboard the USS *Arizona* remain within. Hit by eight aerial bombs, explosions tore apart the ship's interior, setting a fire that raged for two days. (inset) The white marble wall at the west end of the USS *Arizona* Memorial identifies all those who perished.

© Allan Seiden

A navy launch approaches the Memorial dock, a 10-minute ride from the USS *Arizona* Memorial Visitor Center, operated by the National Park Service. The outline of the ship's bow lies just beneath the surface, time slowly eroding her superstructure, gradually releasing the fuel that remains on board, revealed as an oily sheen floating on the waters adjacent to the USS *Arizona*.